LAKE FOREST LIBRARY

P9-CPW-685

LAKE FOREST LIBRARY
360 E. Deerpath
Lake Forest, IL 60045
(847) 234-0648
11/06

WRITE NOW™

A Kid's Guide to Nonfiction Writing™

Writing to
EXPLAIN

Jill Jarnow

The Rosen Publishing Group's
PowerKids Press™
New York

Published in 2006 by The Rosen Publishing Group, Inc.
29 East 21st Street, New York, NY 10010

Copyright © 2006 by The Rosen Publishing Group, Inc.

All rights reserved. No part of this book may be reproduced in any form
without permission in writing from the publisher, except by a reviewer.

First Edition

Editor: Frances E. Ruffin
Book Design: Emily Muschinske

Photo Credits: Cover and p. 1 (boy) © Tom Stewart/CORBIS, (girl) © Jose
Luis Pelaez, Inc./CORBIS; p. 5 © Gabe Palmer/CORBIS; p. 7 © Digital
Stock; p. 9 (bat) © ANT Photo Library; p. 9 (birds) © Corbis Royalty Free.

Library of Congress Cataloging-in-Publication Data

Jarnow, Jill.
Writing to explain / Jill Jarnow.— 1st ed.
    v. cm. — (Write now : a kid's guide to nonfiction writing)
Includes bibliographical references and index.
Contents: Writing to explain — How encyclopedias help to explain —
Outline to explain — Writing a report — Fun resources — Writing lists to
explain — Explaining a historical event — Using contents and index pages
— Proofreading a report — Words that help to explain — Glossary.
ISBN 1-4042-2833-0 (library binding) — ISBN 1-4042-5320-3 (pbk.)
1. Report writing—Juvenile literature. 2. English language—Composition
and exercises—Juvenile literature. 3. Exposition (Rhetoric)—Juvenile
literature. [1. Report writing. 2. English language—Composition and
exercises.] I. Title.
LB1047.3.J375 2005
372.62'3—dc22
                                                2003024461

Manufactured in the United States of America

Contents

Writing to Explain

Are you writing a report about why dinosaurs became extinct? Are you writing a report about how the **American Revolution** happened? Many **assignments** require that you tell how and why something happened. This is called explanatory writing, or writing to explain. For a project that requires you to explain something, it is important to research, which means to gather facts about your subject. Start with library books, magazines, newspapers, and the Internet. Take notes, then write an outline, or plan, to organize your report. Double-check your notes to make sure that the facts are correct.

Reports That Explain Checklist

- Use encyclopedias, library books, newspapers, magazines, and Web sites to research your topic.

- Make and organize notes.

- Make an outline.

- Look for fun resources, such as zoos, science or history museums, or special research libraries.

- Proofread your report.

- Use explanatory words.

Using Encyclopedias

Encyclopedias are great sources of **information** for your report. An encyclopedia is a book or a set of books that lists topics, or subjects, in alphabetical order. A set of encyclopedias has a special **index volume.** The index tells you in which book and on which page to find a topic. An outline at the beginning of each article tells how to get the information you need. The outline may list more articles about your subject in other books in the set.

Check It Out!

Encyclopedias can provide information about special topics. There are encyclopedias about people, sports, animals, science, and weather.

The Encyclopedia of Asian Animals

Tiger

Topics in encyclopedias have a title, which is usually the name of the subject.

The tiger is the biggest and strongest member of the cat family. It can grow up to 9 feet (3 m) long, and can weigh up to 660 pounds (299 kg). Tigers live in the grasslands and forests of Asia. Their striped coats provide them with the cover they need while hunting for food. Tigers live alone, unlike lions, which form large family groups. Tigers have a loud roar, which can be heard from 2 miles (3.2 km) away. Tigers are good swimmers, and they sometimes climb trees.

Scientific name: *Panthera tigris*

Distribution: India, Manchuria, China, Indonesia

The encyclopedia article provides information and important facts about a subject. An encyclopedia article is a good example of writing that explains.

64

7

Writing Topic Lists

If you need an idea for the topic of a report, write a list. Write down your thoughts about the assignment. This can open up your mind to new ideas. For example, if you are writing a report about the habits of wild animals, a topic list will help you to choose your main topic. Write down questions about wild animals. Which animals hibernate, or sleep, in the winter? Which animals migrate, or move to warmer places, for the winter? Then look up the terms "hibernate" and "migrate" in an encyclopedia. Make a list of animals that hibernate and migrate. Choose an animal that you think is an interesting topic to write about.

Topic Lists: Hibernate or Migrate

Free-tailed Bats
Hibernate

Geese
Migrate

Animals That Hibernate	Animals That Migrate
Bears	Monarch butterflies
Free-tailed bats	Geese
Snakes and reptiles	Ducks
Woodchucks	Arctic terns
Chipmunks	Gray whales
	Caribou

Making a topic list can help you to choose an animal that hibernates or migrates.

You might write a report that explains why some animals do not migrate.

An Outline to Explain

Writing an outline is the next step in writing your report. Writing an outline is a way to organize the main ideas and details, or extra facts, of a topic that you want to include in a report. Use the notes that you have gathered from your research to create your outline. First write an **introduction** that explains why you are interested in the subject. Then write the body of your outline. Ask a few questions that will be explained with interesting facts. The conclusion of the outline notes the end of the report. Readers should know the "how" and "why" of a topic by the time they have finished reading the report.

An Outline That Explains a Science Report

I. **Introduction**

II. **What is hibernation?**

   A. Which animals hibernate?

   B. **What happens when animals hibernate?**

   C. **Which animals do not hibernate?**

III. **Conclusion**

Create an outline on hibernation.

Now that you have completed your outline, you can write a well-organized report that explains.

Animals That Hibernate

by Jerome Harris

Many animals hibernate all winter. Hibernation is a kind of sleep. Most bears, brown bats, woodchucks, chipmunks, and reptiles, such as snakes and turtles, are some animals that hibernate. Hibernating animals look almost dead, but they are not. They do not eat, but they are breathing and their hearts are still beating. Deer, rabbits, some squirrels, and foxes do not hibernate. Animals hibernate to live through the cold of winter months.

I. Introduction

II. What is hibernation?

II. A. Which animals hibernate?

II. B. What happens when animals hibernate?

II. C. Which animals do not hibernate?

III. Conclusion

Writing a Report That Explains

A report that explains a topic has three parts. It must have an introduction that explains the main idea of a topic. This is usually the first **paragraph** of your report. The introduction should capture the reader's interest so that he or she will want to read more. The body of your report includes paragraphs that explain the information and that give details about your topic. Each paragraph should have its own **topic sentence** to explain the facts that are in it. The last paragraph serves as the conclusion. It should sum up the facts and details that you wrote about your topic.

Explaining a Skyscraper's Foundation

The Foundation of a Skyscraper
by Beth Morris

A skyscraper needs a strong foundation. Without a foundation, a skyscraper could sink into the ground or fall over.

To make a foundation, builders dig a large hole into the soil until they reach a hard layer of rock. Then builders add columns made of concrete or steel to the foundation. The columns will help to support a very tall building.

Foundation builders often add a "bathtub" to the foundation. It's not really a bathtub but a structure that makes sure water from rain or floods cannot get into the basement.

When a skyscraper is completed, the foundation is the lowest level of the skyscraper. This space can be used for parking, shopping areas, and tracks for subways, which are underground trains.

Introduce the main idea. This report talks about the foundation of a skyscraper, or a tall building.

Arrange your paragraphs in order so that the reader can easily follow the ideas in your report.

Write a strong conclusion, or ending, that describes the purpose of the subject.

13

Fun Resources

Look for unusual, fun **resources** that will make an explanatory report come to life. For example, to check out the differences between turtles and tortoises, go to a zoo or a science or natural history museum. Call the zoo or the museum to see if it has research libraries that are open to students. If you are writing a biography, or life story, about a famous person, he or she may have a childhood home, a museum, or a library that is open to visitors. Many topics have a museum or a library **dedicated** to them. For example, a museum or library may be dedicated to art, music, or history topics such as the **Civil War.**

Visiting Teddy Roosevelt's House
by Cary Mead

Today our class went on a field trip to the home of Theodore Roosevelt. On our visit we learned about how people lived during the 1800s and the early 1900s.

Theodore Roosevelt was the twenty-sixth American president. People called him Teddy. We visited a large house on East 20th Street in New York City. He was born there in 1858, and he lived there until he was 14 years old. A guide from the National Park Service gave us a tour of three floors of the house. The rooms had beautiful furniture, wallpaper, and paintings from the 1800s. Teddy's bedroom was in the back of the house. It was called the nursery. Teddy had asthma as a child. It made him short of breath. His father built a room behind the house that had equipment for physical exercise. The exercise helped to make Teddy strong. On the ground floor is a room with important papers and many photos of Teddy, his family, and other famous people.

Looking at a famous person's clothes, toys, furniture, family pictures, and important papers can help you to explain how that person lived.

Telling people the resources you used to write your report will allow them to visit the source themselves. It also shows that you have done your research!

Using the Contents and Index

To find out whether a book has the information you need to explain a topic, look at its table of contents and index. Nearly every **nonfiction** book has a contents page. This page is located just before the first chapter of a book. It lists the title, or the general topic, of each chapter. It also gives the number of the first page of each chapter. This information lets you find and read the chapters that relate to your topic. An even faster way to locate useful information that explains a topic is to check the index. The index is located at the back of the book. The index lists the book's topics in alphabetical order.

Using the Contents and Index

Imagine that you have to do a report about mountains. Here are the contents and index pages in a book about the Alps.

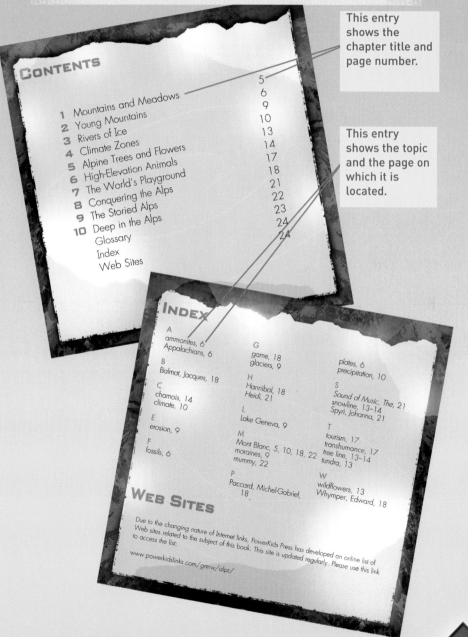

This entry shows the chapter title and page number.

This entry shows the topic and the page on which it is located.

CONTENTS

INDEX

WEB SITES

Due to the changing nature of Internet links, PowerKids Press has developed an online list of Web sites related to the subject of this book. This site is updated regularly. Please use this link to access the list:

www.powerkidslinks.com/gmrw/alps/

Proofreading a Report

Proofreading your explanatory report is part of the writing process. Before you hand in your report, read it carefully to check your spelling, **punctuation**, and **grammar**. Edit your sentences so that they are clear and easy to read. Fix any spelling or other mistakes. Does your report have an introduction, a body, and a conclusion? Mark all the changes on the first copy of your paper. Make the changes, then proofread your report again before you hand it in. The next page shows a report with a few proofreaders' marks. You can learn more about proofreaders' marks in a dictionary.

Proofreading Your Report

Clara Barton
by Lila Douglas

There were four older children in Clara's family. Clara Barton was born in North Oxford, Massachusetts, on December 25, ~~1921~~ 1821. Her sisters and brothers really loved their little christmas baby.

When Clara was 15 years old, she got a job teaching in a one-room school. She taught a of class 40 students. Some of the kids were bullies. Clara won their ~~they're~~ respect by reading a sermon from the a Bible. Clara cared for soldiers in the civil war. In 1881 Clara started ~~a of~~ the American Red Cross. She had become an American legend when she died on April 12, 1912. stet

This first sentence is out of order. Begin your report by introducing Clara Barton.

Study proofreaders' marks in the dictionary, and use them to proofread your report.

Be sure to reread your report carefully before you hand it in.

ℂ paragraph		⊙	period
⤶ remove words in sentence		stet	stet = keep words
L lowercase		⊔⊓	exchange the position of words or sentences
C uppercase		the ∧	insert
⌣ close up			

Transitional Words

Reports that explain need **transitional** words. These help you to move smoothly from one part of your report to the next. For example, use words such as "then," "before," "during," "after," "meanwhile," and "next." These words tell the reader that there is a connection between two parts of your report.

By the time you have written your report, you will understand the facts well enough to explain them in your own words. Writing a report that explains helps you to learn!

Glossary

American Revolution (uh-MER-uh-ken reh-vuh-LOO-shun) Battles that colonial soldiers fought against Britain for freedom, from 1775 to 1783.

assignments (uh-SYN-ments) Jobs that have been given.

Civil War (SIH-vul WOR) The war fought between the Northern and the Southern states of America from 1861 to 1865.

dedicated (DEH-dih-kayt-ed) Given to a purpose.

grammar (GRA-mer) The rules of how words combine to form sentences.

index (IN-deks) A list, usually found at the end of the book, that states what is in the book and on what page it can be found.

information (in-fer-MAY-shun) Knowledge or facts.

introduction (in-truh-DUK-shun) A beginning part that explains what is going to follow.

materials (muh-TEER-ee-ulz) What things are made of.

nonfiction (non-FIK-shun) Writing that is about real life.

paragraph (PAR-uh-graf) A group of sentences about a certain subject or idea.

proofreading (PROOF-reed-ing) Reading something and marking the mistakes that need to be corrected.

punctuation (punk-choo-WAY-shun) The use of periods, commas, and other marks to help make the meaning of a sentence clear.

resources (REE-sors-ez) Supplies or sources of energy or useful items.

topic sentence (TAH-pik SEN-tens) A sentence that tells what the subject of a paragraph is about.

transitional (tran-SIH-shuh-nul) Referring to a change or a passing from one thing to another.

volume (VOL-yoom) A book that is part of a set or series.

Index

Web Sites

Due to the changing nature of Internet links, PowerKids Press has developed an online list of Web sites related to the subject of this book. This site is updated regularly. Please use this link to access the list: www.powerkidslinks.com/wnkw/writexp/